Graduation

Cheryl **Caldwell**

KPT PUBLISHING

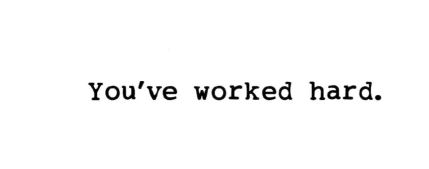

I is
a
student.

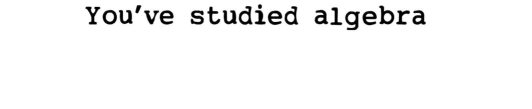

You've studied algebra

If I have 10 cookies,
and you ask me
for 2,
how many
cookies
do I have
left?
That's right. Ten.

and geometry

Dear Geometry,
I don't know what your
angle is, but you're being
obtuse.

—even when it felt
like busy work.

Dear Algebra,
   Quit asking us to find your X. She's not coming back. We don't know Y.

You've studied english,

writing,

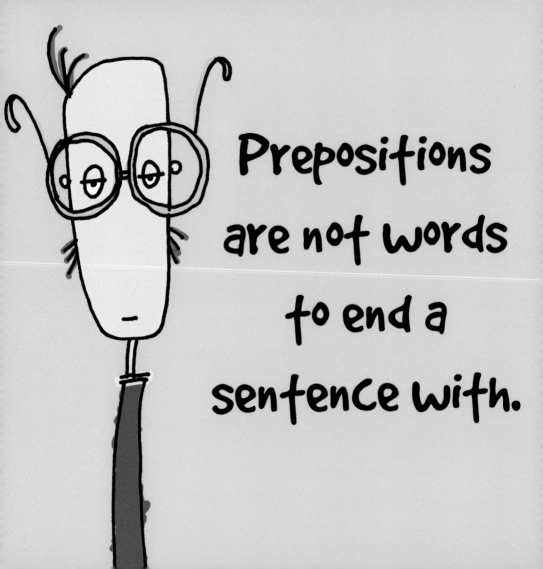

literature,

and science.

You participated in class,

did your homework,

My teacher said my homework was a piece of cake... so I ate it.

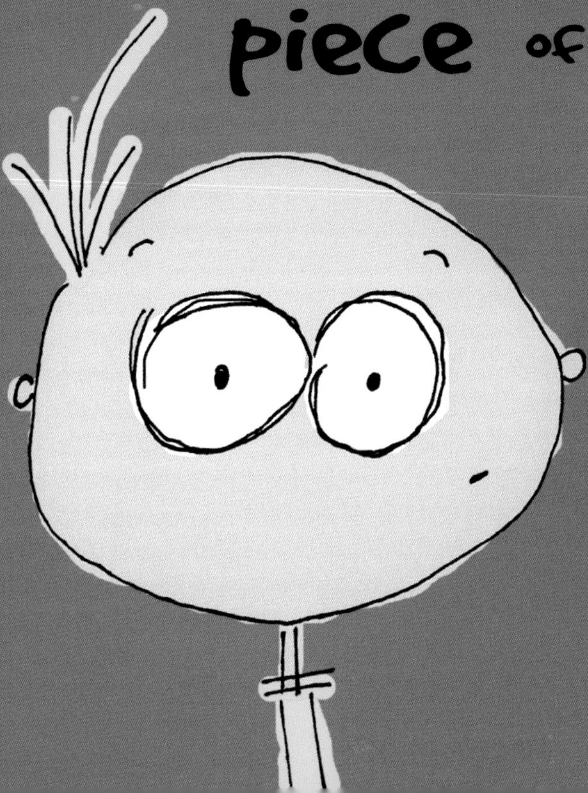

and gave presentations.

If you can't convince them, confuse them.

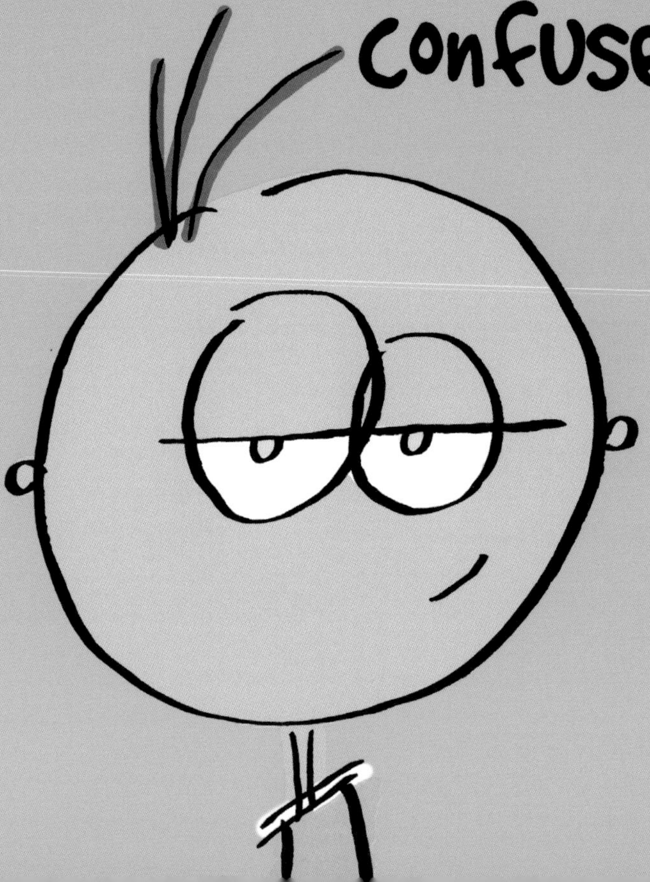

Now what?

I ask kids what they want to be when they grow up because I'm looking for ideas.

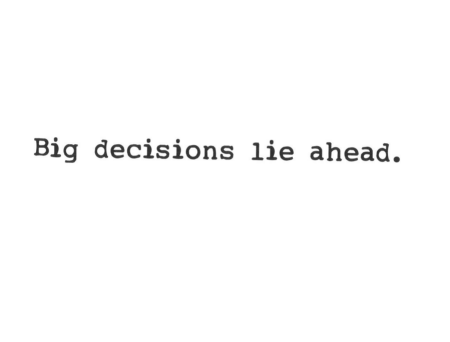

Big decisions lie ahead.

If no one comes back from the future to stop you, how bad could the decision really be?

They say to follow your heart

"Do what you love, and the money will follow"

Binge watched a TV show, ate some ice cream, and stayed in my PJs all day.

And now I wait...

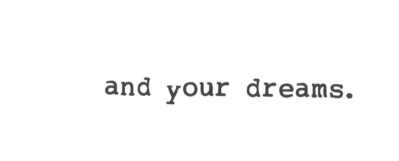

and your dreams.

Everyone will have something
to say about your future

and your bank account.

I just signed up for text alerts from my bank. They text me my daily balance. I love it, but I don't think it's cool that they put **LOL** at the end.

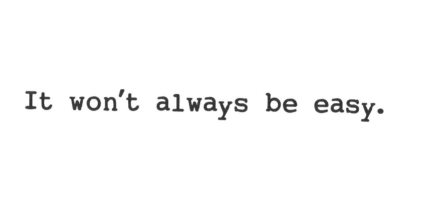

It won't always be easy.

I've given it a lot of thought, and I just don't think being an adult is going to work for me.

Things won't always
go as planned.

If
life
gives you
melons...
you might be
dyslexic.

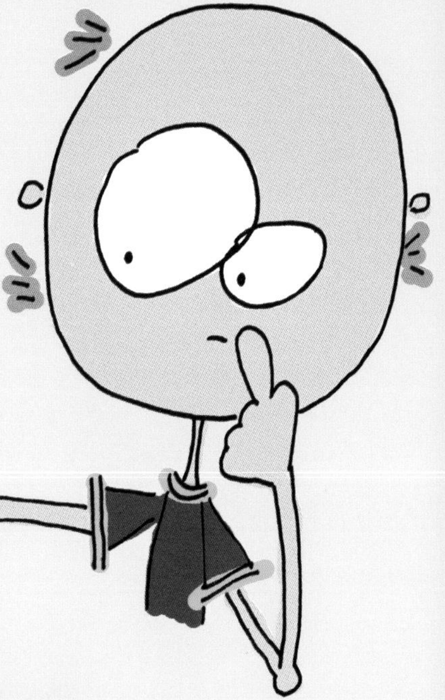

And opposition *will* happen.

But you know who you are
at your core.

Ironing boards are just surfboards that gave up on their dreams and took the first job that came along.

Don't be an ironing board.

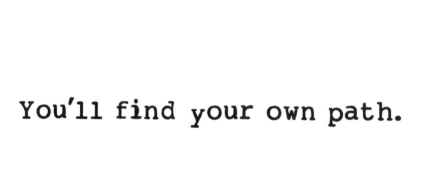

This could go
either way

So for today, celebrate.
Because, yep,
that just happened.

About the Author

Cheryl **Caldwell** is a sometimes artist, photographer, filmmaker, marine aquarist, and author. Most of her inspiration comes from her unconventional view of the world and the fact that she finds the mundane hilarious. She is owner of Co-edikit®, a humor-based company that pairs comical illustrations with a witty combination of clear-cut, down-to-earth words of wisdom and sarcastic humor. Her artwork and characters have been licensed and sold throughout the world. Her original paintings of the Co-edikit® characters can be found in several art galleries in the U.S., including Bee Galleries in New Orleans. She still subscribes to the philosophy that if you're having a bad day, ask a four- or five-year-old to skip. It's hysterical.

Graduation

Copyright © 2018 Cheryl Caldwell

Published by KPT Publishing
Minneapolis, Minnesota 55406
www.KPTPublishing.com

ISBN: 978-1-944833-44-2

Design and production by Koechel Peterson and Associates, Minneapolis, Minnesota

First printing April 2018

10 9 8 7 6 5 4 3 2

Printed in the United States of America